G000094541

DELAYED BY ROUGH SEAS

David Hodges

Delayed by Rough Seas

ISBN 0 9533222 46
Acknowledgements
Spirituality and **The Merton Seasonal**
in which some of these poems first appeared

Published by The Abbey, Caldey Island,
Tenby, Pembs. SA70 7UH, Wales, G.B.

Delayed by Rough Seas

Delayed by Rough Seas

The Celtic, pilgrim, sailor saints
set out to find the promised land
in open boats
of skins stretched out on wood:
the Cross and just themselves
was all they carried.
Carrying within their hearts
the God they sought;
exiles for the love of Christ,
they hoped to reach their true home.
Mystics, no longer longing for
an earthly homeland but for
that unattainable other world,
mythical island, Land of Promise, hidden
beyond the vastness of the sea.
Speaking the universal language
of Christ's love,
birds, all nature, joining
in their psalms and chanting,
singing praise to their creator God.
Hunger and thirst they knew,
knowing heaven's fullness.
Their sails full set and flying
through the sacramental sea,
or becalmed and drifting,
shipping oars and trusting
to the providence of God.
Sailing by the stars,
encountering demons,
storms without, within;
what was important was the journey,
delayed by God to teach them secrets
of the ocean, their inner lives.
Fearless they braved the angry sea
but still they feared the final journey
we all must travel to God's presence,
into the dark unknown, alone.

1

Seascape:

View from a Ruined Hermitage

The tide far out
across a sea of endless sand,
framed by ancient rocks
and far off hills of muted blue,
a trackless, empty space
where small things flourish,
shells, sea creatures,
signs of life in miniature.
A vast stage for wading birds,
for redshanks, curlews,
the red-necked phalarope;
for terns and gulls,
the arctic skua.
Above, a flash
of heron grey
speeds on
across the silver sand;
and white against the light,
a line of gannets
low across the distant sea.
A wild place,
untouched, remote,
and all at one
a hymn of praise,
a place of prayer
and elemental wonder,
a place of peace and stillness,
broken only by the cry
of distant birds,
the whisper of the wind.

St Govan's Chapel.

Stone steps
from the cliff head
in the grey light;
into the cleft
tucked tight,
grey stone chapel
hugging naked rock,
humble cell
and holy well.
The sea air,
the hermit's thirsting
heartfelt prayer
to the hidden God
who's somehow near:
in psalm
and sacred text,
in the single shaft
of early light,
in the quiet sound
of small waves
breaking.

Uncharted Harbour

'Let us not look forward. Nor back.
Be cradled, as in a swaying boat on the sea.'
Friedrich Hölderlin, "Mnemosyne"

Will I forever
anchor in unknown harbours,
never sighting
familiar shores?
Once there was excitement
as the new and unfamiliar
unfolded,
strange lands took shape.
Now the inevitable disappointment
at the weary and unending search,
the same landscape repeated
in harbour after harbour
with finite variations;
always hoping for a sighting
of once glimpsed,
nearly forgotten, shores.
Vague memories
of the harbour of enchanted childhood,
remembered dreams
of lost innocence.

Then slipping anchor, out of harbour,
unnoticed on a morning tide.
Once more alone,
but this time a lighter rigging,
a letting go,
in harmony
with the wind and murmur of the sea,
the waves now slowly catching
the rhythm of some other life,
obeying some eternal motion;
quietly sailing into that longed-for,
uncharted, promised final harbour.

Sea Change

Out in the dripping darkness
the sea is black and deep in thought,
its depths impenetrable.
At dawn, emotion in its heavy waves
below a bruised sky.
Daylight displays the force and power,
the breakers and the spray;
until the midday calm and sparkle
of the summer sun
begins to heal the inner world,
tranquil rim
along the blue horizon.

The Sea, The Sea

Who would live
far from the sound
of water and the gull,
from boats and ropes,
the smell of the sea
and the salt air?
To be at one
with the ocean's sigh,
the breakers and the spray.

Who would live
and not be wakened
by the lap of water
on the shore,
by the sound of the tide
pouring back through shingle,
by the cry of the gulls
riding the sky,
and the creak of wooden boats?

Who would live
and not be entranced
by young seals
basking on the rocks,
by peregrines
hunting the cliffs,
by the sparkle of the sunlight
on clear water,
or the tide come racing in
like lace upon the shore?

Who would live
and not be enthralled
by the sight of white tops,
by the lashing of the ocean waves,
or the sound of the surf
booming in the sea caves
and come crashing in
upon the wild and rocky shore?

And then at nightfall,
be at one
with the stillness,
black and deep,
with the calming rhythm
of the tranquil sea,
a pool of silver
in the moonlight.

Nature Notes

Sunrise, the ritual moment
the ancient archetypal play
enacts; the pure event,
when dark gives way to light.
Gulls dance and golden water
laps the crystal sand.
The soul shivers; the day breaks
like sacred music
arising from the depths of being.
The indescribable reverence
of early morning sounds,
the hesitant cry of the first bird
now taken up by others,
as the tidal landscape
replaces the dark and silence
of the still retreating night.
The stars give way, the cosmos
attunes to a new day.

A Winter Sunset

A red gel orb,
fiery liquid
dripping red,
sinks beneath
a sea of angry blue.
The red sun slides
below the ocean's rim,
pulsing light
and fire on water.
And in the afterglow
of bright refracted light,
appear uncharted oceans
set with islands
in the sky.
I seem to sense
some strange
new other world
that draws me there,
that touches
deep within,
felt somehow
through distances
that seem so near
yet far,
on some other shore
the other side
of silence.

Cathedral Caves

In the deep sea caves
hollowed out by wind and tide,
facing the setting sun,
you who have borne the storm's force,
the sea's anguish now forgotten;
at the cave's mouth
I see you sitting on rocks,
ringed in black,
deep caverns hidden from view,
your figure
lit by the setting sun,
an outline only,
your eyes and mouth obscure,
the coolness of the now stilled waters
lapping the rocks,
caressing your naked feet.

Under Different Stars

Time is running
but oceans separate,
mountains divide.
What are your silent words?
What does your heart sing?
What do your thoughts embrace
in solitude?
As we sleep
under different stars,
I give my message
to the rising moon.

Windswept Isle

Broken dry-stone walls
and huddled cattle,
the rusted fence,
the straining gate,
the muddy windswept pool,
flayed by pulsing,
horizontal squalls.

After Rain

My senses sharpened
to the earth's smell.
After the brutal rain,
nature's intimacy,
everything once more alive,
insects, birds emerge.
The silver birch
its shimmering leaves
now joyfully trembling
in the gentle breeze.
In the silent forest,
a faint memory
of a distant harmony
drifting on the wind,
evocation of passing time.
And the rain falls softly
once again.

The Wildness Within

'Don't you know yet? Fling the emptiness out of your arms
into the spaces we breathe; perhaps the birds
will feel the expanded air with more passionate flying.'
                    Rilke,
              "Duino Elegies 1"

The wonder and delight
of wilderness,
the wild places,
landscapes
that feed the soul,
satisfying other
deeper needs,
nourishing
the inner emptiness,
the infinite inwardness,
of human longing.
Spiritual loneliness,
expressed in endless hunger
for ineffable horizons;
desire for
infinite freedom, eternal love,
stifled
by the drab and everyday.
Who can trace
the flight of birds there?

The wildness within,
the untamed centre
that cannot be contained,
released
by letting go;
opening out
to something greater,
something other.

Touching the void,
utter Beauty
the soul alone can sense,
beckoned
by some distant music
from some celestial sphere,
some eternal landscape
the wild fire within
embraces.
Afire with desire
for God.

Wilderness

Wilderness weather,
a lull in the
unforgiving
horizontal rain.
The seascape boundless,
rugged headland
after rugged headland,
the peregrine hunting,
gulls riding the wind.
The soul stiff with cold.
Dusk comes quickly.

The Peregrine Hunting

From out of the sun
and silver sea,
the peregrine hunting;
fierce, magnificent,
wide wings winnowing,
swiftly beating,
fast and deep,
sweeping the bay,
overtaking its prey.

Wings back,
shooting like a bolt,
a swish through the air,
bullet-faced diving,
stooping, driving
its death-administering claws;
the heart freezes,
the gull dropping,
the peregrine checking,
swooping for its kill.

At the cliff edge,
the sharp 'kek-kek'
of the peregrine's whickering cry.
How small and ugly now,
with wings drawn in,
about its ordinary business.
No longer terrible,
no longer beautiful,
in the tearing of flesh
and the funereal feathers
drifting.

Oystercatchers

Watching, waiting.....
grouping, black on white,
and rising
into the clear, clear air,
to form a line,
an arcing, whirring line,
to skim the surface of the sea,
the sea like glass again.
They hold my gaze,
smaller, smaller,
pulsing, throbbing there.
Willing them further, further...
Deeper, deeper into prayer...

Hawk Hovering

Through the winter-wind-bent trees,
a watery light, silver on black,
against the grey and cloudy dawning sky,
the hawk hovering, beckoning the day.

In the silent chapel, bent and praying,
cowled and hooded monk before his Maker,
struggling in the dawning darkness
till the ecstatic 'prayer like fire' arrives.

*(John Cassian's 'fire prayer':
ecstatic prayer of contemplation)*

Red Kite

Sailing, soaring high,
gliding light and free,
forked tail and angled wing,
the red kite wheeling,
hanging like a crossbow,
checks, then plunges
through the silent air.
Beneath
the fir-fringed mountain,
the blue lake
reflecting back
the sky.

Still Life

At the still point
both of solitude and silence,
still unexpected, the light of grace:
watching while the sun comes up,
shining through leaf and bark,
falling speckled on the earth.

Listening
to the world awakening,
catching my breath in wonder.
Still finding no answers,
but learning to ask
better questions

What is Red?

Red is vibrant, pulsing
Colour of the setting sun
Red is for danger
Passion, red-blooded rage
Colour of life and death
Blood on the casualty floor
Red flag, revolution
Colour of fire and heat
Red-hot, flame and scarlet
The dress a young girl wears

Lipstick, blushing for shame
Strawberries and summer wine
A field of poppies
Geisha and ripe cherries
Red roses and flamenco
Grand Canyon and Ferraris
Cinema seats, red velvet
Cricket balls, old London buses
Red hair, fox fur
The redwood tree

End of the spectrum
Simply red

Blue

Blue is sky and sea
Azure blue, Prussian blue
Dark as midnight
Flax in sunlight
Cornflowers
Colour of eyes, baby blue
Blue ribbon, butterfly's wings
Hedge-sparrow's eggs
Lavender blue
Ice-blue, steel blue
Cold and deep, navy blue
Kingfisher-blue
Turquoise, ultramarine
Sapphire, electric blue
Rainbow hue
Colour of Earth from Space
Union Jack, national blue
Blue in the face, blue blood
Out of the blue
The blues

Yellow

Sand, canary, Chinese yellow,
Saffron, peach and straw,
Jonquil, jasmine, melon,
Sunshine, blonde and lemon,
Honey, butter, corn-on-the-cob,
Apricot, buff and golden-haired,
Amber, dandelion, primrose,
Sunflower, buttercup and crocus,
Brimstone, Sulphur,
Citron, ochre,
Old gold, wedding ring,
Mustard, custard,
Daffodil, sunrise,
Halo, crown and sovereign,
Tan and gilded-gold.

As if anew

Almost in awe, I watch
the dawn's grey morning twilight
touch the silent lake;
the soft still air, cool
before the day's first brightening.

Breathless I watch,
as the earth's sap rises,
all nature awakening;
and the forms and shadows
divide and part,
hazy shades of green and grey
piecing together
the shape of a new day.

Daybreak brings a chill wind;
and I shudder
at the piercing clarity
of texture and form,
as if anew.

In the Interval of Waiting

If once so subtle music,
one note soft and clear
from some eternal sphere,
breaks through in time.
If words are formed
as yet unheard
to awe and to delight.
If things are shaped
of beauty yet unseen,
evoking something other.
All earthly sense suspended,
withdrawn from time
in deepest silence;
the core of being
for an instant only
opened,
then tight closed.
To find the the soul's smile
brought forth clear shining
on soaring flights of love,
the fruit of struggle
welded out of seeming chaos;
once more saving truth
and beauty for a time,
fragile index
of our world's survival.

Silent Interval

Bright stars
Frozen trees
Silence

Falling snow
Cold grey
Solitude

Monos

I am content
behind these walls.
There is no sentence passed
beyond a vowed intent.
I no longer hear
the once familiar sounds
of city streets,
but merely see
the tops of trees,
the distant sea,
the passing flight of birds,
the changing pattern
of the stars, the steady
progress of the sun.

Freed to trace
an imaginative space,
drawing features of
an inner landscape,
echoing the eternal.
I am no more
the job I once did,
defined now more by being
than by doing, no more
confined by my enclosure.

Psalm 118 *

And the sky turned black
while we were singing
'Your word, O Lord, forever
stands firm in the heavens'.
Then out of nowhere
lightning struck,
thunder struck,
the heavens broke,
the power was cut
the building shook,
surrounded by white light.
The heavens emptied
and hail showered,
thick as snow,
while we continued
(without a break
for goodness sake)
singing praise
to God most high,
in awe and trembling
at His
almighty power.

* Caldey Abbey church 27/ 2/02
8.55 am, Terce

29

Enclosure

Enclosure walls
and silent windows,
light and shadow
in the sun's hot glare.
The inner courtyard,
cloistered shade,
tranquil rest,
where small birds nest
and flowers gently open.
Enchanted joy
to heal the inner soul.

Lectio

Cold sunset
Open window
Listening to
the wind

Open book
Sacred text
Drinking from
the hidden spring

Lectio (2)

The Spirit falls;
words rise from the page,
joined
like doves ascending.
My spirit rises,
lifted up
into the Word.

Holy Scripture

Let me lie down
among your words,
find shelter there,
roam and browse,
lie down and ruminate,
taste your sweetness,
as you reveal your
hidden secrets
to me.

Feed me and restore me,
fill all my longing,
let me play there
at your threshold,
let me drink deeply
from your healing spring,
from the river
of your delight.

(after St Augustine)

Held Within His Love

In the early morning watch
the eye begins to see,
through shuttered windows,
slowly breaking light
shaped from the silent air,
breaking through the chaos
of the dark;
lighting a new way
when all creativity
seemed dead, and
something missing in my heart.
Yet nothing now is lost, when
freed to enter once again
the sacred untouched space;
a light and gentle wind,
a sea of silver light,
and love held out
to catch
my faltering step beyond.

Epiphany

When a burning, shining,
dancing light,
imprisoned in darkness,
escapes its horizon.
When life outleaps its limits,
enters into the unknown,
sketching out the possible
lyric truth.
Like sacred music,
something as yet unheard
bursts forth,
like a shard of absolute beauty
refracted into this present
imperfect world,
breaking through boundaries,
holding open the space
between conscious
and unconscious thought.

A space is cleared,
something new survives
of the ineffable divine,
of beauty drawing to itself;
but then returns us,
too soon seemingly abandoned,
to aching consciousness.

Journey Without Maps

Trust to enter
on the longest journey,
from head to heart.
Confront the geography
of past memories and fears,
only trust your heart
to penetrate the dark,
to bring the unacknowledged
shadows into light.
Find every sorrow healed,
every fear erased,
imagination cleansed,
transfigured by love.
Place of joy and beauty,
of mystery and longing,
for the soul's uplifting.

God is Near

My heart
harder than stone,
drier than the desert,
jaded,
wearied of all taste,
wanting
to be nourished
by your sweetness,
cleansed of all but you,
refreshed by your delight,
filled by your beauty
and your goodness.

Source of love and being,
far beyond thought,
yet 'even at night
directs my heart',
captivates my soul,
clasped to you
like an eaglet
to an eagle's wings,
like a tree
surrendering to the wind.
Source of inner life,
above the shouting chaos.

Even sadness
suffers change.
Dawn finds
a single bird
piping for the rest.
Something just suggested.
God is near.

Snatched Words with a Lover

Now when prayer
seems dry and empty,
seeming best avoided.
When all that's left is
like a drawn out
one-way conversation
with someone
you still love;
all communion
felt as broken,
out of touch
but aching
in the lonely desert
of the heart —
how did we get
to this?
Not the way
we started,
excited
snatched words
with a lover.

Then the metaphor
breaks down.
Prayer obeys
no normal rules
or explanations.
All that's left is
just the will to pray,
when all is
dry and empty,
persevering
dry as tinder
in that shared and arid
time and place.

Until the sudden
startling
prayer like fire
arrives,
and all is new again:
shared heart, shared spirit,
like, but unlike,
the thrill of
the first excited
snatched words
with a lover.

The Spiral

All things recur,
unchanging rhythm
centred on the self,
until the circle grows,
becomes a spiral.
Then love goes outwards,
believing it is loved;
progressive movement
to the summit,
infinite desire
is met
in God.

Reaching Out to Love

Acknowledge the love
that leads
and feeds us.
Happiness unlocked
by giving
not by getting,
not by having
but by being.
Acknowledge the love
burning forth to draw us;
restless hearts let go,
surrender
into Love.

The Olive Garden

His suffering heart
cruciform, overcome
with maternal love
at all the trials
and depths of evil
we must meet.
The burning forehead,
the runnelled face,
the eyes etched there
with sorrow.
How wide the heart
and womb that shaped us!
His suffering caused
not by fear
but loving mercy,
tortured by compassion,
agonised by love,
His sweat as drops of blood.
Justice turned to mercy there,
love turned all to gentleness
through depths
of tender mercy.

(after John of Ford, c.1140 - 1214)

Wrestling with God

*'And Jacob was left alone. Then someone
wrestled with him until daybreak......'*

Genesis 32:25

Abyss of light,
abyss of dark;
questing,
seeking for truth
in God and self.
Always just
beginning to define
an authentic whole.
Spirit and flesh
at war within,
struggling for meaning
but longing for union.
Wrestling with God
and hoping to lose:
and to pronounce
with utter truth
'Not my will
but Yours'.
That final harmony
where all resistance
ceases,
where all is taken up
into a greater
all-embracing love.
Coming to peace
with God and self,
in morning mercy's
gentle light.

Mystic Bridge

Love, the only bridge
there is to cross
between eternity and time:
suspended over
the abyss of nothingness.

Christ, the bridge,
absorbs our sin and hate,
transforms us into love,
his arms stretched wide for us
between eternity and time.

His wounded hands
beckoning, calling us
into our place reserved:
to risk the journey into
the circle of self-giving.

Resurrection Life

Broke into uncreated time,
made a pathway for the Spirit,
when He died and rose:
brought us into unity
with Him and with the Father
and each other.
From suffering brought peace,
turned sorrow into joy.
All guilt and shame
and hate embraced,
transfigured by His love.

The hope of all our longing,
united with the Father's will,
sharing in that same Spirit,
the love of Father and of Son
now flowing to us,
source of love indwelling
allowing us to echo,
if we dare,
'not my will, but yours,
be done'.

Mary

Quietly uttering
Her earth-shattering
'Yes'
Virginal readiness
For God's Word
Lovingly willing
Fount of self-giving
Faithful, fruitful
Mother of God
Purity of heart
Stillness of soul
Confident the Word
Was meant for her
Nourishing
Breasts of peace

St Luke

Your Gospel of mercy and forgiveness
showed us the Prodigal Father,
arms outstretched,
running out to meet us in his love;
the Good Samaritan,
how we should love our neighbour.
You showed us this God of tender love
in the human heart of Christ.
A Jesus who shut the door on no one,
from birth he sought
to be among the lowly,
concerned for the marginalised,
the outcast and the stranger.
But quick to challenge
those attached to wealth, the proud,
the grabbing, hypocrites, the insincere.
He showed great love, respect for women,
and a preference for the poor.
He came to save the sinner,
he came 'to seek and save the lost'.
It was His concern that all be saved,
a Gospel of repentance and forgiveness
for all the nations of the world.
He loved, forgave, up to the end:
'Father, forgive them
for they know not what they do'.
His forgiveness absolute,
his mercy boundless.
Even in death,
ready to welcome us back
with wide open arms.

Mark

'Who do you say I am?'
A Question Mark,
racing for the finish,
And at once...And at once...
immediately, in a rush.
Powerful drama
of the Good News
of the Reign of God
in Jesus,
of the Kingdom
close at hand.
The heavens
were torn open,
when God proclaimed him
as his Son.
A mystery,
a gift for us,
baptised for us,
anointed with the Spirit,
driven to the desert
to be tested
and defeat the devil,
dispelling darkness,
breaking chains.
The Son of Man
who came to serve,
not to be served,
a model
for those among us
who would be greatest.
Yet he was revealed
as Son of God
in words and mighty deeds
of healing, feeding,
calming storms
upon the Sea
of Galilee.

He challenged, awakened faith,
cured by touch, confronted evil,
preached conversion,
was obeyed by unclean spirits,
aware of who he was.
A Christ who ate with sinners,
questioned
the established order
symbolised by Sabbath
and by Temple;
denouncing hypocrites
and those who piled up
human regulations.
Taught with authority
a teaching that was new.
Gave us a New Commandment
to love our neighbour
even as ourselves.
Mark gave us
the mystery
of Christ's person,
of Jesus, Son of God
but Man of Sorrows.
A suffering Messiah,
born to suffer
and to be rejected.
The paradox
of losing life
to save it.
Obedient love:
Not my will
but yours be done.
The Crucified
and Risen One.
Love that gave himself,
His Body and His Blood,
to us in bread and wine;
mystery beyond
Mark's question.

Dewi Sant *

David, patron of our land of Wales,
chief of the saints of Britain,
three symbols foretold your birth:
salmon, stag and swarm of bees:
abstinence from all but water,
power to trample on the ancient serpent,
and wisdom, words of honey.
From childhood famous for your miracles,
restoring life, reviving sight,
you healed the blind Paulinus.
You built an abbey at Glyn Rhosyn,
now St David's, with your monks.
Known as 'the Waterman',
you lived on bread and water,
cress and wild leeks.
You placed the yoke upon your neck,
used no ox for ploughing,
obedient and silent,
austere, long hours in prayer,
your community of love
transforming life in Wales.
Made a bishop, then archbishop;
by Jerusalem's Patriarch given gifts
of bell and staff and altar,
a tunic of woven gold.
You founded twelve monasteries,
established fifty churches,
throughout the west of Wales.
On the way to Brefi,
you restored to life
the dead son of a widow.
At the Synod, the earth rose up
beneath your feet
so all could see and hear
you preach the word of truth
to defeat Pelagius' heresy,
who denied original sin.

The dove upon your shoulder
a symbol of your wisdom,
you were declared Wales' primate
by all assembled, kings and bishops.
At your death you told us:
'Be joyful, keep the faith,
persevere in the little things
you have heard and seen me do'.

d. 589

St Gertrude the Great of Helfta: Herald of God's Loving-Kindness *

Tenderly she wrote
of his mercy and compassion,
and the loving-kindness
in the heart of God.
Favoured by ecstasies and visions,
but disciplined by grace,
she made quick progress
in the school of love.
By her accepting trials
in union with Christ's passion,
loving others till it hurt,
suffering healed,
enlarged her soul.
Her life was rooted
in liturgy and prayer,
was sanctified by joy;
captivated by God's beauty,
she was transfigured
by his love.

Love's excess,
impetuous desire,
her will became a fire
to liquefy her soul,
poured out in offering
to her gracious Lord.
Bride of Christ, she had
such passion for her lover,
in her heart
she was imprinted
with his holy wounds.
By this he healed her soul,
gave her the cup of love

then, sharp like an arrow,
came the wound of love.
She joined her whole will
to his firm embrace,
melted Christ's heart
by the heat of her heart;
in her heart
his heart found repose.

1256 - 1302

St Teresa of Avila *

Mystic, Doctor
of the Church,
she kept her common sense
and humour,
despite those many visions
and often inconvenient
levitations:
all that tying down
her legs in choir.
Remembered
for that angelic wounding
and exchange of hearts
with Christ.
Christ spoke to her
in rapture
in her depth of soul;
next she saw him
in his risen form.
And then an intellectual
vision of communion
with the Trinity
in light.
She was told:
'Don't try to hold me
in yourself,
but try to hold yourself
in me.'

She taught us to enter
an Interior Castle
made of diamond
in our depth of heart,
where we reflect
God's image
and his likeness.

A castle made
of many rooms,
where in the centre
secrets pass
between the Trinity
and man.
And, reader, note
the door is prayer;
but reptiles,
toads and vipers
guard the outer court.
It's sin that makes
the diamond black,
but God is even present
when the soul
is not in grace,
in the most interior,
in the greatest depths.

Of prayer, she taught:
'It is for you
to look at him.
He never takes
his eyes off you'.
The Lord himself
became her 'living book'.
Prayer for her
was drawing water
from the well,
but only God provides
the rain.
She taught that prayer
is intimate sharing
between friends;
taking time to be alone
with him we know
loves us.

Then surrender into
the arms of love,
for prayer
is such a tight embrace,
until the soul is silent,
the soul in God
and God in it.

The soul,
of which the silk-worm
is an image,
takes life through heat
coming from the Holy Spirit.
It spins its silk
in prayer;
dead to the world
but hid in Christ,
it comes out a butterfly.
Death, new life in Christ.
The soul itself
in rapture,
drawn out
of all its senses,
given gifts,
experiences of God,
but yet not forgetting
the mysteries
of Christ's life and passion,
'dwelling on them still
with simple gaze'.

The butterfly in flights
of restless love,
but strange
as though in torment,
not in joy.
The soul is blind and deaf,
not understanding union.

With rapture intermittent,
the suffering soul endures
until the soul is purified,
until desire increases.
Then we're told
that in some place
very deep
the window of the intellect
is opened;
from the soul's eyes
God removes the scales,
the vision of the Trinity
revealed.
In all simplicity
the soul made one,
connatural, with God.

In union
all thoughts pass away,
all faculties are lost,
when we become one flame
with him,
the stream that merges
with the sea.
But this too is intermittent,
and takes place within
the very depths of soul,
this overwhelming
experience of
the reality of God.
Now on the surface
all is calm,
one's whole being
totally centred
on the Will of God.
In every present moment
completely free and able
to help fulfil his plan
for us.

This union now bears fruit,
as witness St Teresa's life,
although God doesn't look
so much at the greatness
of our works
as at the love
with which they're done.
In Teresa,
this spiritual marriage
bore fruit
in renewal of her Order,
in writings
and in new foundations,
by her death fourteen.
This meant travel
throughout Spain.
She spoke of
stubborn mules,
bad drivers;
but she travelled
with her gaze on heaven.
Life on earth,
she said,
is but 'a bad night
in a bad inn'.
Our reward
is God himself:
'Let nothing disturb thee,
all things pass...
God alone suffices.'

1515 - 1582

The Cistercian Martyrs of Tibhirine *

Martyrs through love,
who stayed to face
the hatred and the pain
but did not die in vain:
forgiving in advance
the assassins they foresaw.
Seven lives transformed,
breaking through death
with selfless love.
Killing hatred,
conquering by tenderness,
dialoguing, making friends
up to the end;
Christian monks
mediating love,
building bridges with Islam.

Now they see
as the Father sees,
all his different children
shining with the glory
of his Son.
Sowing seeds of peace
and reconciliation,
seven lives given
for God
and in solidarity
with the Algerian nation.
Praying that
one day too
we all may see
the face of God
even in our enemy,
who can then become
our friend.

* *Christian, Luc, Christophe, Michel,*
Bruno, Célestin and Paul,
assassinated 21st May 1996

Mary and Son

Thrilled,
surprised by joy,
heart on fire,
chosen pure vessel,
transparent to
God's light and power.
Obedient love
freely conceives
the Word
she heard.

Mother of the Word
made flesh,
whose flesh
she had given,
whose flesh
she had borne.
Mother of Love,
now changing hearts,
hearts for giving,
hearts for sharing.

Emmanuel, God-with-us,
to make us
one again with God.
Here to teach us
God's love
and loving kindness.
Here to fill our hearts
with wonder.
Here to scatter darkness.
Here to bring us light.

A life lived out
in sacrificial love,
fully revealed
upon the Cross.
Dying to redeem us,
to give us grace to save us.
Inspiring us
to imitate and follow,
to start to turn life's sorrow
into endless joy.

Ground Zero

'Beauty will save the world.'
Dostoievsky, *"The Idiot"*

If truth and goodness
are distorted
and the beauty
of the cosmos marred,
who will answer
for the silence of God?

But the world will be saved
by beauty; touched and healed
by beauty seen as love,
where love and beauty meet
in truth and goodness,
in the shadow of the Cross.

Breaking through evil,
transforming it to good, by love
like that enacted on the Cross.
Divine love outstretched,
Christ drawing us
to imitate his selfless love

In sharing and compassion.
In all our pain and struggle
to break the chain,
forgive the unforgivable.
In love for enemy as well as neighbour,
Christ's power breaking through.

In the courage
of the rescue workers,
in their unconcern for self.
Despite our rage and sadness,
the shock of joy
in response to good.

In the drama still
enacted daily at the site,
in the active loving kindness,
in the prayers now offered
beneath that towering
mysterious Cross.

Light will once more illumine darkness
through unconditional forgiveness,
through pure uncalculating love,
the distorted image
healed and deified
by the uncreated grace of God.

Death in the Afternoon

'Death in the afternoon'
was the title
of the last essay
he set,
just before
they found him dead
in his flat,
in a pact
with his girlfriend
dead opposite.

We were told
at assembly
that he'd left a note,
but not what he wrote,
just he'd left
the windows open.
Pray they left
the windows open
in heaven.

[True story. Happened when I was 16. I'm still praying.]

On the Threshold

When I was young,
I ran unthinking
down that path.
Joy breaking out,
a light heart,
the hand held out
for giving
and for living.

Looking for
that other self,
a mirror for my soul;
shy wonder in my eyes,
love not yet discovered.
Just the faintest echo,
yet inviting,
like a far off sound,
playing on the threshold.

Something
always about to happen,
yet never happening,
exquisite,
yet unfulfilled.

These are but Shadows Cast

All I have left
I give you:
what tears unshed
I give you.
Too many things
I left unsaid:
how I have felt
the separation
and the passing years,
so cruelly tearing
apart the memory.

When we met
it was too late,
too late
for what I'd planned,
rehearsed.
The still raw wound
unhealed,
in that hidden place
between remembrance
and forgetting.

For what is past
forgive me.
For what we've missed
forgive me.
Perhaps we could begin
to bypass others' hate,
make good the loss,
build up with love
what hate tore down?

These are
but shadows cast
when all is lifted
to the light of God.

Undigested Traumas

Full of undigested traumas,
angry, bitter, unforgiving,
full of guilt and pain,
bitterness unsoftened,
reconciliation refused.
Angry memories harden,
so much business unfinished,
so much tension
festering relation.
What can into this
release forgiveness?
What can into this
bring wholeness,
love again for him, or her?
Why not imagine Christ
forgiving you
for the worst thing
you have done,
and then imagine Him
forgiving him, or her,
through you?

The Meeting

Building bridges,
unlocking memories
time has not healed.
Not now open wounds
but deep scars remain
over a gentle heart.
Fruit of suffering embraced,
transfigured by love,
borne without bitternesss;
a door swings open.

Finding a smile,
a friendly gesture,
words unrehearsed,
words shaped in silent prayer.
Now building bridges,
unlocking doors,
defrosting hearts,
finding joy
to drive out sorrow.
Eyes open to see miracles.

Where Joy and Sorrow kiss

'Joy and woe are woven fine,
A clothing for the soul divine'
William Blake

All our lives
pick up the threads
of joy and sorrow,
matching silks entwined.
The more of one,
the more the other,
but joy eclipses sorrow.
Far, far better then
to suffer
than to not have loved.
Grief is the price of love,
and in our grief
we can reach out
to others' pain.
If in this
we see the hand of God,
then all our lives
of interwoven
joy and sorrow
make a tapestry of love.

Life Goes on in the Compound

Flies are buzzing.
Foreign correspondents taking pictures
just to let you know

where that bag of rice you paid for
went. Send another soon:
life goes on in the compound.

Mum died giving birth to No 3;
now sister makes my bowl of rice.
The TV crews have gone.

Every day under a sky of tranquil blue
life goes on in the compound.
But sister lies asleep:

'No more rice', she said.
No one now unsticks my eyes.
Will life go on in the compound?

Sustainable Growth

When we've developed
all we can develop,
when there's nothing left
to JCB,
when we've taken
all there's left to take
and given up on giving,
will the bubble burst?
When consumerism's hollowed out
society from the inside,
exposed a void
devoid of meaning,
while politicians try to kid us
that yet again
they have postponed the evil day,
will spin still cover up our sin? —
will speculators still gather
like hungry crows?

Third World Terror

That night I had a dream
of all the world's armed forces
mobilised and on the move,
swathe on swathe of 'planes,
fleet on fleet of ships,
all bound for my country
and others near our blighted land.
Then, in terror, I awoke
to hear the 'planes descend
and drop their heavy cargo,
darkening our skies....
but there was no sound of bombs exploding,
just cries of joy and of thanksgiving.
It was all the food
and all the other things we need.

Water Aid *

Brilliant exercise
in lateral thinking;
India's untouchables,
below the lowest caste,
restoring precious water.
Hand-picked and trained,
to mend once idle
broken water pumps.
Breaking down
ancient barriers
with bicycles and spanners.
Despised, rejected,
now respected
in every village.
Allowed to touch
what before
they could not touch;
allowed to share
the common cup.

* *The Charity*

Top Shop

Will the world become
a wall-to-wall mart,
with shopping taking over
all our culture?
Will all our youth
be offered as a sacrifice
to this new Mammon? —
as fashion victims
scrabbling feverishly to find
that extra something
they've been told they need to have,
together with providing
cheap labour
for his ever bigger shrines?
When will we release them
from this bondage,
from the endless misery
into which we've tricked them,
into which we've held them bound,
to feed and please an adult world?
Or like Abraham with Isaac,
when will we grasp
the solution by the horns,
refuse to wear
designer labels,
and force our advertisers
to target the adult ram
rather than the lamb?

Hotmail

Wherever in the world
are you?
How on earth
are you?
Why do I have this
printed e-mail,
but with no address
I can reply or fly to?
Perhaps it's just as well?
Perhaps I just wanted you
for what I wanted you to be?
In this terrestrial network
what a star you are!

'Delayed by Rough Seas' *
(The lament of a delayed Caldey letter)

You can never,
or hardly ever,
rely on the Caldey mail-boat
being at a time you can quote,
or, if there's a wind or a squall,
even running at all.
It's a sure bet that I can
be there and back to Japan
before you could send me
from Caldey to Tenby.

To their detractors
they'll say there are factors
like the moon and the tides,
but there's lots more besides:
there's the rise and the fall
at the harbour wall,
there's cold fronts and warm fronts,
high pressures, low pressures,
there's the neap and the spring,
all affect the boat's crossing.
Of course they'll cancel without fail
if there's a force nine gale,
but little more than a breeze
in an easterly direction
will find all of us seized
with vast fits of depression,
and a big wash or swell
all optimism dispel.

Even if the weather forecast
is neither windy nor overcast,
you'll find no one committing
beyond 'weather permitting'.
Some will rely
on what they read in the sky,
others on what they can spy
in the boatman's eye,
but you could be here years
and be ranked with the seers,
and your chances would still be remote
of learning the mystique of the Caldey boat.

So tie me to a pigeon
unless you can use your religion,
instead of praying the psalter,
for walking on water.

** Stamp which appears on the Caldey mail
if the boat fails to run*

Our Father

Our Father
of the Universe,
just, merciful and loving,
help me to realise
that it is *my* greed,
the size or my engine, my wardrobe,
my wallet, and my grocery bag,
that causes the exploitation in the world;
that I am responsible
for the structures of oppression;
that it is *my* failure to share my daily bread
that causes malnutrition and starvation;
that it is *my* lack of forgiveness,
my harbouring of resentment,
that causes hatred and division;
that it is the violence in *my* heart
that causes war.
Father, forgive me, help me to forgive others,
and to realise my need of their forgiveness.
Help me to realise that you are *our* Father,
not just *my* Father, Father of all,
not just of those of *my* colour, *my* race
and *my* religion,
and that we are all equally your children.
Establish your kingdom, where your will is done,
where everyone is free and freed from need.
Help me to denounce all structures of sin.
Save me from hypocrisy and spin.